Alone:

With my thoughts

Author: Stefan Bercea

Page intentionally left blank

Introduction

In the span of seven days, life can transform in profound and unexpected ways. It is a week that can leave an indelible mark on one's existence, shaping the course of their journey in a manner they never envisioned. This book invites you to delve into a week-long odyssey, a fictional exploration of emotions experienced while awaiting a life-altering diagnosis.

Each chapter represents a day in this emotional rollercoaster, a week in the life of our protagonist, whose journey is a mirror reflecting the very human emotions we all grapple with when faced with uncertainty and adversity. Although this story is a work of fiction, it is inspired by the real-life experiences of many who have had to confront chronic illness.

Throughout this narrative, the author, inspired by personal experiences, will intermittently engage with you, dear reader, to provide insight, raise questions, and invite you to ponder life's deeper questions. The author does not intend to be a guide, but rather a fellow traveller on this path, offering their own perspectives and vulnerabilities, with the hope that you may find resonance in your own life's journey.

As you embark on this seven-day adventure, you will witness the protagonist's evolution, from denial to acceptance, through various emotional landscapes: avoidance, pain, depression, guilt, and isolation. It is a journey punctuated by highs and lows, much like the rhythms of our own lives.

In the bonus chapter, we extend an open invitation to the realm of philosophy. We implore you to ponder, reflect, and explore your own philosophical musings, for philosophy is not confined to ivory towers but is an integral part of the human experience.

By sharing this narrative and inviting you into a world of introspection, we hope to provide solace, empathy, and perhaps even a glimmer of hope to those who have travelled a similar path. This book is a testament to the resilience of the human spirit and the capacity for transformation, even in the face of adversity.

Abstract:

The bonus chapter, as promised, is a gateway to philosophy and introspection. It is a call to action for you, the reader, to engage in a philosophical exploration of your own. It is an opportunity to delve into the deeper questions that life often raises.

In the pages that follow, we present a series of philosophical questions, scenarios, and prompts. We invite you to take your time, reflect, and navigate your thoughts and questions that these prompts elicit. There are no right or wrong answers here, only the opportunity to engage with your own thoughts and beliefs.

Philosophy is a journey of the mind and spirit, a quest for understanding and meaning. It is a process of questioning, challenging, and evolving our perspectives. This appendix is a canvas for your philosophical reflections, and we encourage you to use it as a tool for self-discovery.

As you ponder these philosophical inquiries, remember that philosophy is a dialogue with oneself. There are no prerequisites or formalities. Your reflections are valuable, and they contribute to your personal growth and understanding.

We hope that you find this bonus chapter a meaningful addition to your reading experience, one that inspires you to continue exploring the vast universe of ideas and questions that shape our human experience. Philosophy is a journey without a destination, a path where the journey itself is the destination.

Thank you for embarking on this literary voyage with us, and may your own philosophical explorations be as rewarding as the journey of our fictional protagonist.

The following table of contents provides an overview of the book's structure, guiding readers through the emotional journey of the protagonist as they await a life-altering diagnosis, and culminating with an invitation to explore the realm of philosophy and engage in philosophical reflection.

Table of Contents

Day seven

– The beginning –

Time stamp 06:50am

It is morning already. Something has ripped me away from my eternal slumber. I call it eternal because it makes me feel eternal. It is the most beautiful feeling which one can ever experience. No dreams, no thoughts, no problems, no pain…… my misery is gone. With no significance in my existence but happy, this is how I sleep. I feel suspended between the abyss of my reality where the world does not confront my ideals and the horrific world in which I have been graveling my feet for the last 8766 days. But nevertheless, I must awake, duty calls, and this world need my meddling. This cluster of pillows surrounding my feet, I barely can move, and I would kill for another minute in coffin of pillows.

What a morning, not even the sun wants to awake, but I have too…. Gladly I have made my tasks easier for this unfortunate day. My attire has been prepared with a night before, waiting for myself to act and start this morning. I will grab it and take it with me in the shower, cleans my body like every ordinary man in under ten minutes. This is what they call hygiene, personal hygiene, an action so simple which has become so complex over the years. How easy it used to be, to have someone assist you in this task. Not a finger I had to lift; no effort was I supposed to put in cleansing my body. What a beautiful begging of life and what a horrendous way to ended. Imagine not being able to wash yourself. You have worked all your life, how long it may be to prove your independence and out of a sudden someone takes it away from you. Let's skip this thought I do not intend to make you sad or inform you that this may be your future. Where were we, yes indeed we were in the shower, but by this time this action has ended, my body is clean, so is my mind. Wiped from all the nonsense which has prepared me for this world. Music, music is the nonsense…… you let it run in the background of your daily task and wipes your mind. It takes you miles away from where you are and lets you see the world through someone else eyes. It sounds good, traveling with your mind in all the corners of this world, it sounds astounding to experience a different world in a matter of minutes. The problem are the interruption and the people which present the world. Let us talk about the interruptions. Music used to be free, it used to come from freedom of expression. Nowadays it is an expression of hunger after money, a capitalisation of needs and an excuse of production. Even if you find yourself into this you will be interrupted by the continuous adds. There is no greater disturbance than interrupting your journey, your feelings. It feels despicable to be ripped out and pull into a commercial asking for your coinage in exchange of a product of no need or interest for yourself. Nevertheless, this train of thought has took me into the kitchen where I stare for what it feels an infinite of moments to my addiction. The poison that keeps me alive through my days, the poison which does not let me return to slumber and pushes me to work. But not this morning this morning is special. This is the DAY; we are not allowed to drink this poison as it may interfere with our endeavour in discovering the sickness lurking in my blood. So, water it is for this morning, just water, no coffee, no poison today.

Oh no, that sound, not good, she is awake. Hopefully, she goes back to sleep. Wishing I could sip a cup of coffee I realise I was mistaken a sound for another and that my quiet morning will not be interrupted by the one I confessed my love towards. Well back to my usual thoughts and fears, kicking me into existence and punching my inner demons back in their boxes. Man, I miss my coffee, there is quieter in my head with sip of that bitterness taste of life. Coffee on its own is the essence of life as I know it, bitter, unbearable, and undesirable until you start to add sugar, milk and all the crazy things one may think about it. This is life is bitter, is needed and in need, and it becomes sweeter when you add things and people in it. Yes, some people may be expired just like the milk, but it is up to each one of us to decide how their coffee will be, encapsulated in an entirety of objects, surrounded by people or simple, clear...... bitter. Well time is off the charts and my appointment is coming soon. I realise I have not informed you of my appointment my dear reader, and this is because I would like to take you on a journey with me over the course of a week. Therefore, next time we see again it will be of a different time and place. More precisely about a week prior to our introduction, but do not worry I will not treat your existence like a dirty mop, yes, I will not discuss directly with you like I am doing now. But I will often interject and leave you crumbs and commentaries from time to time until you are back in present time, on point for my appointment.

Day one

– Denial –

Time stamp 11.00

Good morning life, what a perfect time to wake up, no work no duties, nothing to do just relax. Perfect way to start this day, shower routine, COFFEE, emails, twitter, news.

An ominous voice disturbing my thoughts "Good morning love" ………… this is where I should draw the line, jump out of bed, strait into the shower, pretend you have not heard her. DON'T SAY ANOTHER WORD "Any plans for today" ………. Well, I had some between the five seconds of being awake and you taking away my independence. I wish I said that, instead it was something more like this "No plans sweetheart, you want us to do something together". Now from here there was some monolog to which I did listed an unimaginable amount of words from someone who has just woke up. Gladly for me I have answered yes to everything, even if there was no question, a YES is much simpler way to end a conversation than a NO. With a NO, everyone demands reasons, and a deeper understanding of your reasons. Let me give you a perspective: "Are you okay?", by giving the answer "Yes", the conversation can move on with no more acknowledgements for unshared problems. In the possibility of giving the answer "No", it invites more conversation, more unwanted attention to problems which are socially deemed as unspeakable, such as the "Why and How". While at the same time exploring the notion of peer judgment or the feeling of not fitting in, therefore it is much easier to say" No" and not explore the pain.

Now back to our fictitious story, after asking permission to complete my morning routine, I find myself in a very difficult situation. My COFFEE has not been prepared, after agreeing onto an exchange of my free time for the rest of the day for a cup of delicious bitter tastefully liquor of dark souls with no fancy sprinkles and just a tear drop of milk, I find out that she has fallen asleep. It took me fifteen minutes to complete my morning routine, the equivalent of almost four songs, and she fall asleep. See I could have thought about anything else at this time, such as the issue of methods of recognising bad policies in institutions which offer therapy for victims of domestic violence, but no I had to think about how our arrangement was betrayed by one's incapacity to wake up. Agreements used to sacred, they had meaning, now in the era of connectivity they mean as much two quarters of a pence. I hope there is nothing wrong with……. A look our coffee is ready, time to bring her the coffee to bed. While at the same time it is important to recognise that my generative thought process is emerging from something which I will refuse to speak off, maybe later, maybe when someone will ask, I'll not answer with a "No" and uncover what I'm feeling. For the moment I choose to live in denial land.

"Honey, I made you a coffee, just as you like it". Discussions, discussions, discussions an unbreakable cycle of wasteful conversations around the same old, unchangeable events, places, and people. Or as others call it, small talk. Part of human nature to discuss rather than act. We all have ideas, problems, needs, thoughts and so on, but very few of us have actions. I think it has been a bit over two hours of somewhat pleasant conversation, it is definitely, the time to suggest that we eat. Maybe I can say something that will make her understand that I would like to take her out for a nice meal. Something along the lines of, should we go out to eat, or maybe do you want to try this place out……… "I'm hungry". That is all that my mouth was able expel, hopefully she will understand. "Do you want me to make us some sandwiches………blab bla la…………… you made the coffee so I'll make us some sandwiches you can come with me downstairs". No, no, no, no, NOO, I have to say something to now "Okay". Well, that was it. Five minutes later: "You told me we can make sandwiches but there is no bread, I thought you had bought bread yesterday when I asked you to buy it. Have you bought the things I asked you? I sent you a list, three times …………………………." There it was, a feeling at the back of my head, I knew I had forgotten to do something yesterday. Who would have known, that remembering what you forgot can feel delightful, so oddly satisfying, just like an accomplishment? Shouts, need to say something! She is starting to look at me "So that's what I forgot to do, I'm sorry, at least I bought you flowers……" a good silly face should go well with this. Two seconds later "That's it you are taking me out to eat". Was it Karma? or "the secret" which said what you stink comes around, or something like this, nevertheless I still get to eat something good in town. While at the same time the mundane has become exhausting, living has become exhausting, and how it could not be. I've spent more time putting my energy into denial land to avoid living in pain that I forget what living all is about. It used to be about all those beautiful and conflictual moments and now is just another day towards the end. Still there is no time for this as the story must move forward.

And this is how the eternal waiting has started. It has been an eternity of unbearable thoughts and processes in my mind. The things I could have done, the time which I have wasted waiting. But should not waiting for the person you love be bearable. Should not it be the most enjoyable time that you can wait. We promise each other love, eternal happiness at good and bad times, and now in time of purgatory I feel suffocated by endless possibilities and lack of freedom. Where, in reality, I've been only waiting for 20-30 minutes. My mind has escaped to the realm of possibilities and forced me to experience an endless delight of unreal scenarios. The wonders of my mind are greatly inexplicable, as for I have escaped the waiting and engage in commuting myself to lunch. But my thoughts are still infected by regret. Regret of something unreal and not mine to have. My thoughts could have been of joy of what I have. A joy of waiting for the person I love, unfortunately, something inside me has made me think this way, with regret and not joy. Time is of essence there for breakfast has become lunch, and lunch must be quick in order to have time for dinner. There are always good thoughts when eating, conversations and reflexions over the recent time which has passed. For eight minutes, the world reverses itself and leaves me with the impression that ages have passed by. Well lunch was good but now it is time to move on, and from now one I see two choices. One I keep thinking and focus on myself and second, I renounce my desires of analysing human behaviour while accompanying my partner in a walk-through town. And just like this a third thought emerges from the bottom of mind saying, do both at the same time. Just as living in denial land and trying my best to keep my normal life untouched by what I'm experiencing. Here we go let us check their walking and there are some oddly fellows walking in such fashion that gravity has been pulling their feet closer. The more I look around me, I see people not knowing how to walk. It is not hard, you just move a foot in front of the other one, at an aquept pace, in a straight line. Nothing hard, but some specimens manage to trip, fall, step on themselves without any effort. Of course, I do recognise signs of effort, struggle after an injury, but those people in front of me, they just forgot the basics of being alive. Without admitting, that might actually, refer to myself, as I forgot the basic of being alive. Nevertheless, we still engage in conversations of mundane topics, and somehow enter a store of cheap clothing. As for my own frustration of such companies that offer inferior quality products at ten times the cost of production could not be higher, there is an incredible number of individuals per metre square. I admit I am shocked of their presence, mostly claustrophobic. I spot with my eye a corner of escape. A corner in which there were another four men waiting. This was my chance to a peaceful and enjoyable waiting. I choose to not wait, I shall name action, damage control, and put my efforts towards informing my partner of the atrocious quality of clothing items. Even better I will show her how atrociously and poor is the quality of this place. And there I go explaining each inch of fabric, the way that it should be sewed in, unfortunately my efforts are in vain. Maybe I hoped that if I can identify something flooded in this system, maybe she can identify something flooded within myself. She chooses to purchase items which she will have to replace in very short period. This is where I realise that others cannot notice pain through abstraction of rational, but maybe through experience, recognition and sharing, maybe. It's time we return home, and continue to enjoy each other company, falling asleep on the couch while watching a movie. It may not be much, but it has been a good day, I feel good that in the end I have manage to offer her a day together. With no disturbances, distractions, and interactions. And yes, I say all the above paragraph to myself before I fall asleep. Well done to me I have manage to deny the pain taking over my body, my essence. I have denied this pain to infect the one I love. As there is nothing more emotionally painful than seeing those you love to suffer from the inability to help someone they love too. Today is a victory. A victory by living in denial.

Day 2

– Avoidance –

Time stamp 16:10

An odd moment to feel awake, for some it might feel near the end of their day, maybe feeling an itchy sensation on their palms and back of their neck…. Yes, the feeling of going home. Unfortunately for me it is the start of another working day combine with mundane commitments of socialising and being involved in others' lives. But first, let me return to my dream, as this is the only thing which I can share to fill in those pages. Quite short and abrupt but still in control, my dream was inside the fire. Just like every other dream which I have had since I was little, I was in control, I have enjoyed the image of fire, surrounding me, not being able to see anything past it. The heat warming up my skin, giving me comfort in the absence of pain and smoke. Of course, it was just a dream, I would never do this in real life, but I 've always felt a good connection with fire or heat. I am not sure if warmth is what makes me feel happy or what allows me to be happy. Whenever is hot enough I feel I can still move on, regardless of pain and struggles converging on my existence. I miss seeing the sun. Now I realise that after working for over a year of night shifts that its presence has given me strength to push through everything. Maybe you my dear reader are not capable of understanding the feeling of "charging". When moving from shadow to sunlight or when it finds a way through creeping upon you when sleeping. For me it has remained the most comforting touch. Going back to this day, coffee, breakfast and ready for work. As some days are not important neither this on. Barely any memory stamp and it will probably be forgotten from my memory just like footsteps are erased on the warm sand of the Black Sea. My sweat memory compels me to embrace it and recall onto the moments crucial to my existence, childhood……

I feel I have escaped being incapable and needy, I feel of use as an adult. My role, my job, my friends, they are proof of my capacity, competence, and incompetence of being alive and independent. Or as I prefer to call it, alone among others who are also alone.

Dreaming what a beautiful exercise of mind, awake or asleep the human mind is never at ease. It always finds ways to dream. When we sleep, embracing fire, when we drink our coffee, hoping for a better future. On the way to work when not listening to music, enlisting fear into our options, or making us reconsider decision and events from our past. Here comes my problem dear reader, dreaming should be involuntarily, and my dreaming is not. I induce my dreaming; I force my mind to dream so that I can feel. So that I can feel what other are feeling. I am an empty shell, maybe just like you, hopefully just like you. And dreams engulf me into a cascade of understanding your ontological perspective of how I should react to mundane events. Mundane events carry the burden of mundane expectation, of normalcy. My normalcy is that things are different, events are different and unique, and people are different. Unique and at the same time mischievous. You expect me to say that they are honest, well they are not. Furthermore, on this subject in a few lines and back to my understanding of normalcy. If I am right, which I mostly cannot say that I have been wrong, then me being unique is me being alone. Not alone without others, or without possession and goals, but alone in thoughts. What does it mean you wonder; it means that I have at least one single idea that no one else has ever thought or will ever think of it. Of course, with this another problem arises. Which idea belongs to my creation, not sabotaged by others which are alive, have lived or will experience life, which idea belongs to me alone. Coming back to your obsession, people being mischievous. They always have been, and they will always be. A child life starts with a lie. Birthday presents, hide in front of a lie, a promise towards happiness is the start of a lie and even hiding the way you live at is a lie. People lie to themselves, to others but especially to those who cannot be seen. I feel it is time for me to end this day, for you it may be too much and for me to little. I promise to consider you in another day, another page and maybe consider sharing with you my only idea.

Interjection

I interject my dear reader,

I hope you understand that this book, my book is neither personal nor real. I hope you understand that it is ……. Thoughts on paper.

I emphasize this book on your understanding my dear reader, and you need to know. You have been chosen to read it. This is the only way in which I can share some thoughts, and not with anyone. With you. Therefore, lets philosophise together.

Understanding is everything in life and knowing is everything in death.

As you will not believe me let me explain to you. We all know, and I hope you do, that the sky is blue. Because we know, now it is dead. There is no meaning in knowing "The why? and "The how?" and "The when?". It comes down to understanding "The why? and "The how?" and "The when?", and that's what brings life to be alive. Going back to our sky, to understand colour, give us purpose. To know the colour of the sky give us an information to store. Can you see the resemblance? Chasing information, being alive. Knowing information, being stored in a box/ coffin. Anyway. You might be old, young or neither but when a child asks, "The why? and "The how?" and "The when?" your knowledge receives meaning, importance…., purpose. Before those questions all your knowing was dead. When someone dies, we try to understand, and only when we understand we can give them value. When you know someone, they are there for granted, they will never leave. Just like parents, or better said, you assume they will never leave. Those are the thoughts we have when others are alive, but after we have lost them, we give value to each, and every action, even the odd and hard to understand. Because by understanding them we keep them and us alive.

I hope you my reader, you can understand. That all we do is to avoid pain. This story is about pain, past, present and future. Day two, is just a representation of how we can choose to avoid pain. We switch between our thoughts, we explore memories, we think of the future. Such exploration of the possible, it is time costing enough to skip a day and not live-in pain. Please, understand that within interjection I'm speaking with you, and you can speak with my thoughts. I'll take you back to day one where we lived in denial and now, we have moved to avoidance. You might already know or feel it, something bad is happening. Remember life moves on, even when bad things happen, and the character is fictitious. Back to denial, pain is a feeling which no one desires. Denial is a first step towards processing pain, regardless of if inflected or being to be inflicted. The knowledge of its reoccurrence on a repeated frequency can make denial a quick decision. Not just for the person in pain, but also for the people carrying for that person. In other words, if you deny its existence, you can prolong the status quo and keep those loved, untouched by pain for a few more moments. Unfortunately, it does not last forever. It does last enough to realise that you can live with pain. Therefore, we can establish a relationship between the person and the feeling. Where the person does not want the feeling, but the feeling does not exist without the person. So, on avoidance as the first step of our relationship with pain, or we might call it the second day in our seven-day journey towards embracing pain. We can reflect on what is to be avoided. The answer for our story is life. Life in pain can be avoided. The modus operandi, or the way in which this can be executed varies from journey to journey. If we might explore, we could at least explore the darkest of them all, suicide. The end of pain, the end of life, the end of agony. It is a normal thought for anyone to have, including our character. Young or old everyone can think, in the toughest moments of life, "How would it be if things were to end here?". For me it is these questions which brings on the realisation of life as being interconnected. It brings into focus that the end of one's life, will and should affect others. From family, to friends, to community in which that individual is living. It might be good to ask and reflect on these questions, as each life in a group of 20, touches and influences the life of 19 others, which on their own shape and mould the life of a community. It might not seem much when living in pain, but it is everything for everyone. Imagine the following though experiment: One person makes a mistake; another comes to support and offer a solution. How many people benefit from this experience? The answer is everyone who can hear about the event/ problem and the solution. The same applies with living in pain, trying to deny or avoid it. Until a solution is shared, listen and acknowledged, life is nothing more than alone. Within finding similarities in each journey and encountered problems we can discover solutions. Now I'll have to let you go into the next chapter, but promise to meet again, for more discussions like this one, bouncing from one idea to another.

Day 3

– Living in pain (Anger) –

Time Stamp: 21:20

Movie night, how should I start. I know I will be abrupt. My thought lingers at why we are watching movies in the evening. But I feel I cannot understand the why, and that is because I have not answered the how. How are we watching movies? Well, there are a few elements involved into watching movies: the time, the set-up and the people watching with us. The time we watch a movie, dictates the movie. Watching a movie before going to sleep influences how you sleep, watching a movie in the afternoon influences your topics of discussion for the rest of the day. That is why taking someone for a movie in the afternoon can dictate the rest of the day. It's amazing how exposing ourselves to imaginary events produces such strong feelings. Certain times will resonate with different movies, such as horror genre with night and action with afternoon.

But what if you have control of the time, and you can watch a movie at any time you want. Well, this is something else. Let us call it a day off. Video on demand services give you control over the time, and you are no longer a subject of social customs. In other words, you are isolated from social interaction. Going to the cinema or watching a movie on television at the same time with everyone who is watching the same channel brings an element of community, of belonging. Watching a movie on your own, whenever you desire brings only control in solitude. Which is the weakest form of control. You must have realised that is easy to choose what you want when you are the only person present, and much more difficult when you must converse with your family. It takes negotiation, patience, and acceptance, for everyone else opinion. Would prolong exposure to solitary dominance and control have an impact on day-to-day interaction, such as lack of body language, strongly opinionated decisions, entitlement, and other side effects…. It is yet to be discovered.

What we know, me and you, is that time is not everything the set-up may be ass important if not more than the time you choose to watch the film. As you can "make time" or shape your schedule to accommodate for movie if it is in the right set-up. Salted popcorn and a drink, big screen and comfortable chairs or your device (phone, tablet, tv, etc.), your sofa and takeaway. Both attractable offers, one socially demanding and the other one socially isolating. Or as we establish previously, offering control. Therefore, the set-up is no different than the time. Socially influenced.

Let us look at the people who can share the joy and sorrow, who experience the same visual representation. They can be strangers, unknown to our customs or friends and family, known to our customs. In our controlled environment where time is not our problem, our choice is not denied, and the set-up reflects our effort for comfort. Would we accept strangers, would we accept the unknown or would we prefer solitude? Interference with our customs/ with traditions is something which is thought not to be taken lightly. It is what make us build walls and give us imaginary rights to judge other. It is unspoken to have different customs/traditions under the same "roof". It is custom to have people who are known, friends / family, invited and accommodated under our "roof" to socially interact / watch a movie. As long as they do not contradict our opinions.

As we can think of, the people, the set-up, and the time they only give us reasons for exclusion or vice-versa. It can be permitted to relinquish control over the time, to surrender to comfort of your couch and to abandon our fear of customs for a more complex experience. Such as living by yourself is a lonely but easy to master life, living with others it is more complex and socially rewarding experience.

Now that we have answered the how, we can start answering the why. Why are we watching movies in the night? Why do we desire to be social before the end of our day? Why do we want do end our day watching imaginary representations of different feelings?

The answer is simple after a long day or week of working hard, putting up with problems, our or others, we are likely to relinquish control and demand relaxation. Regardless of the how, "How things are going to be achieved", relaxation, peace, laughter, and joy are more desirable after a long and rough journey. The more problems you encounter the more sweater and precious your rewards will become. I am not saying that the movie industry thrives on your struggles, but maybe other industries are. For the movie industry has more honest and simpler history than politics.

Therefore yes, we watch movies to entertain our dull lives but there is more. We engage ourselves in isolated or social behaviour to respond to our needs. When overwhelmed, we isolate. When alone, we look for comfort. Just like a pendulum we swing from one end to another. Present the audience with fictive realities some closer and others further away from their reality. The audience, we, you, me and others, gain control, perspective and understanding beyond comfort. Just like with any social activity you get communities, rebels, opposition, and outsiders. This further creates borders, and codes of conduct, defines acceptable and unspeakable.

Therefore, yes, we watch movies because it is embedded in our society, but there is more. Where do movies start? They do not start at the play button, neither at the idea of writing the movie and neither at the actors portraying the characters. Movies start with childhood, they start with the act of playing, recreating, imitating, imagining, and creating. They start in the solitude of our thoughts, and the collaboration with others close to us.

Therefore, yes, we watch movies to complete our childhood, to extend our playtime and imagination. But this is not complete. The complete reason is that movies or any other social activity executed outside of work-related activities is executed with the purpose to restore balance. Balance to our social norms, which we have establish at the begging of our journey, balance towards the unfairness of the social norms which were created before our time and balance towards our busy and mundane routines.

The escape, the sweet apple now either in solitude or with other, now explained for my understanding. With my thoughts exposed now I accept and surrender myself to watch a romantic comedy with my partner. Regardless of how bad it was my day. I have not been in her shoes. Therefore, I accept this sacrifice and relinquish my control for her to choose a movie.

Acting upon my anger, from my encounter with pain has brough me exhausted. At this point in time there is no need to continue, to pursue any more thoughts, feelings, or emotions. It is better to immerse myself into the movie and forget of my chaotic and painful day. What kind of pain are we talking about? Where it is the kind that lashes out. The one that crumbles your body. The one that has been persisting for ages.

The struggle has never been the pain. The struggle is to not hurt those around you. The most inconceivable action which no-one wants to inflict but eventually manages to do so. Pain from illness affects those around visibly more than those who are inflicted physically by it. In its essence, the host of the pain struggles in a perceived fight to not expose his true feelings to those around him. It is the fear of change. Of those loved changing from their normal, happy state, change by affliction of noticing pain.

Day 4

– Depression –

Time stamp 02:30

Why don't I sleep?

Why am I awake when everyone else is asleep?

My thoughts alone do not allow

My mind alone cannot escape

My soul is trapped into my carcase

It is me, alone and cannot escape

Could it be another who infringe on my ability to sleep?

Could my beloved invade into my dreams?

Could I be forsaken of her love?

Could I be forgotten from her memory?

Is it just me, or the night brings more questions for the following day?

Is it just me, who wonders on connections?

Who misses the opportunities of the past days?

Who seeks solutions and answers, into oblivion?

Am I alone into my night?

Or surrendered by unknown?

I write to you, you read from me,

My desperation remains empty.

The words above are just my thoughts,

The thoughts before an empty mind

I clear it now......

Now I am at peace,

I cannot sleep in peace.

The planet cries, and cries like me,

Without a gram of empathy

You rest your head and go to sleep,

Your brothers cry, your sisters mourn,

You rest your head and go to sleep,

The elderly decide your fate,

You rest your head and go to sleep

Without a gram of empathy.

I will try again, to clear my mind

Clear it is, clear, like it is mine

This world is cruel, I must admit, alone it is the reason I cannot sleep. From the day we are born until the end of our lives, we grow customs of separations, of being alone. Your place to sit, your room to sleep, your toys to play. No different than your borders to protect, your options to vote and your taxes to pay.

Silence for you as well.. and me.

Interjection

You must apologise to me!

My dear reader, why don't you listen? I've wrote to you and you alone, that I work during the night. Now you have read the words above and assume they were my thoughts. How dare you break our trust, to assume such nonsense is mine?

It is ours, or better said it's yours. Your problems, your cry of humanity, your plague on planet earth and your lack of communication.

I was busy doing my role, and you dare to imagine that everything I say is real.

This is a book, a guilty pleasure, your time for relaxation and mine of reflexion.

If you leave now, after this scold, remember this piece of advice. Words mean nothing compared to actions, therefore never believe anyone's promises, not even yours.

Because you stayed, I'll tell you one more. My meaning was to stop you, to forcefully stop you, to think, to process and to be sure. If you have stopped for one moment alone and gave meaning to my thoughts, answering my questions, then those have become yours, your questions, your answers, your thoughts, forever yours.

I hope you've experienced a moment of frustration, "How dare a book addresses me and asks for an apology" kind of a moment. I needed you not only to understand but to experience a jolt of anger. Within embracing pain into everyday life anger or better said frustration is part of everything. The source of frustration is undoubtedly the magnitude of pain expressed physically, emotionally and socially. The latest (socially expressed pain) is the one we are most interested in. As we don't live isolated from other just like us. We interact, and we make choices according to our interactions and limitations. Upon being burdened with living with chronic pain our behaviour changes and until adaptation kicks in we can notice an increase level of frustration. Such overcharge of emotion is possible to overload even the most basic and simple activity, such as watching a movie, expressing an opinion, asking for salt. I'll try to give you an example based on our discussion. Imagine watching a movie, when the pain starts, it feels like your organs are being repeatedly smashed with a hammer inside of you. Physically, upsetting, uncomfortable, demanding of screaming and deserving on being frustrated on the situation itself. Emotionally, overwhelming, with the ability to transcend any activity (watching a movie) that you were doing, it takes over and redirects all your attention towards feeling in pain. Socially, perplexing and paradoxically forcing you into hiding your pain from those you care about. Socially demanding control over your painful condition and exerting autonomy over your reaction. Biologically you are in pain, emotionally overwhelmed but socially attempt to pretend that everything is okay. We will refer to this condition as untroubled waters. The surface level must appear unchanged, unhinged of the disturbance/ movement underneath. Reasonably this condition cannot last, as there is movement under the water (pain) and there will be those around noticing. It is upon realising that those close to us are affected both socially and emotionally by our condition that pushed our relationship with pain from avoidance to anger. Anger is a process of consumption and consuming. It is consuming to be frustrated on living with the pain. Physically and emotionally demanding and socially exhausting to pretend that you are okay. While at the same time is it fuelled, similar to a fire that never dies, kept alive by adding small branches, arguments, events, contradictions, etc. The phenomenon of consumption maintains the relationship at the stage of anger indefinitely or until the process has been consumed. Upon being consumed it transcends rapidly into depression. A long-lasting period of low mood which affects your daily life. As per my attempt to exemplify in day 4 the impact of depression, rapid changing thoughts, sleep deprivation, negative thought production, persistent attempts of clearing negative thoughts, failure to recognise it as depression etc. On the bright side, this is just a book, and it only lasts a day. We have accelerated through those stages of living with pain, as the person experiencing the pain is awaiting news on his condition. From the beginning of day one in this book, we have seen the evolution of getting closer to certainty. The certainty that this unbearable pain, described above as hammering internal organs is chronic, life lasting and it will never go away. In reality it might be more than a seven-day journey, depending on how swift the medical system can act. Without any further discussion I ask of you to continue reading into day five and day six, hopefully meeting my thoughts at the end of day six.

Day 5
– Guilt –

Time stamp 7.40

A guilty night, I just woke up. Is there a purpose to my day? All I can feel after such night and knowing what is to come, is that I'm guilty. Guilt must come from something, but never be expressed directly. It lingers and creeps out from my depression, from my sadness of what is supposed to come. While at the same time it transports me back into my childhood where I can re-live all my guilt accumulated over my entire life. It is my fault I've started it, down the rabbit hole of sadness, guilt has pushed my morning into spiral. Luckily, no one else is aware, and I may be able to hide it for one more day. Rather than dealing with what I see as my mistakes, I choose to improvise a plan. This plan should hide my sorrow, from those around me. Those who might suffer from my suffering alone. While eaten by guilt, never have I thought that sharing my suffering with those who care about me, might be normal and healthy, not just for me but for them as well.

Bye, bye morning routine, welcome the madness of guilt, chewing nails, pulling hair, tapping feet and rubbing eyes until you realise. To avoid discussion on a subject, you must distract with different subject. Mission setting: asking others to do or engage in conversations which are only time consuming and delay discussion on your pain, in the hope the day will pass. I was told that humans are creatures of care and concerns. They are, and the worst are friends, close friends which replace blood family. Such family, (created through pure friendship, and not assigned at birth) does not deserve to be saddled with sorrow. In moments of imminent illness, of death knocking on the door, and especially on awaiting decisive news on your health, you might choose to keep them uninformed. It is the sorrow in their eyes, their incapacity to act, their realisation of their own limitation growing. While my freewill is turning into dust and therefore prevents me from sharing my pain, my guilt with them. Who would ever want to cause even the smallest amount of sadness, well my guilt is telling me that by sharing I would cause devastation. I realise now that humans are creatures of wavering thoughts and semblance. In other words, they look for similarity in what they experience with their past, and doubt based on what they accepted to know as truthful information.

My action has been set in stone, today my aim is to act, distract and divert my close ones from even thinking that I'm in pain. I cannot perceive to fail; I can only imagine them being happy and untouched by the pain I carry alone. Before I start to act and pretend all day, that everything is okay. I have one though which I must cast away: "If I act this way, do they act the same as me". My behaviour, choices and actions are learned and emulated from others behaviour and actions. If I choose to go down this route, I choose to acknowledge that others might be in pain, just like myself. A comforting thought, but unwelcomed in my mind, as I risk assess the danger in this thought there are two avenues. This thought presents, uncertainty, lack of knowledge a fifty-fifty possibility of being true or false. If true, I cannot accept it to be true, but if true it means that by sharing my experience of pain with others, I would be no different than them, it would not hurt them and it would make me feel normal. The risk of this being false is that by sharing, I would be different, possibly estranged from their mundane lives and cause them sadness. Take the risk? No. I cannot afford the risk. I can, I will continue to deceive them, and tell them that I'm okay. Might try, no, I'll succeed in making them laugh. Better with a smile on then with a sad thought in mind.

Day 6

– Isolation of pain –

Time stamp 12.50

In a world that felt increasingly isolating, I found myself yearning for an escape from the overwhelming solitude. The constant barrage of notifications and the persistent hum of technology had left me emotionally drained, and I longed for peace and quiet more than ever. I had a plan – a desperate attempt to escape from the digital confines that seemed to be pushing me closer to the edge. With a heavy heart, I turned off my phone and left it behind. As I ventured out into the world with nothing more than the clothes on and some cash in my wallet, the absence of my smartphone gnawed at me like a relentless, nagging void. My mind was a swirling tempest of anxiety, haunted by the notion of unread messages, missed calls, and the creeping sensation that I was growing more and more isolated. But I pushed those thoughts aside, determined to break free, and headed towards the nearest bus stop.

I boarded the first bus that appeared, without any specific destination in mind. I asked the driver to drop me off at a random location, and that's precisely what happened. As the bus started moving, I couldn't help but, for the first time in ages, I felt truly alone. The bus traversed winding roads, passing through serene landscapes and quaint villages. Each new stop drew me further into a world that was a far cry from the constant chaos of my everyday existence. The villages were quaint and picturesque, with their charming cottages, peaceful gardens, and welcoming locals who waved and smiled as I went by.

Time seemed to blur, and before I knew it, it was 12:50 – the moment I had chosen to commence my solitary journey. I had brought a packed lunch with me, and I found a secluded spot by a tranquil stream to eat. The solitude was palpable, and I revelled in the gentle rustling of leaves and the soothing murmur of the water. It felt as though my worries were being lifted, piece by piece. As I continued my aimless wander through the countryside, my thoughts turned inward. Without the constant distractions of my phone, I had the space to reflect on my life and my choices. Leaving the digital world behind had opened new avenues of self-awareness. I began to understand that I had been ensnared in an unending cycle of work, social media, and obligations, leaving me overwhelmed and utterly isolated from my true self.

The villages I encountered along the way felt like hidden sanctuaries, untouched by the breakneck pace of the city. I engaged in conversations with the locals, absorbed by their stories, and even assisted a farmer in repairing a fence. Time seemed to stretch and bend, and I cherished every moment of this leisurely day. Yet, despite the beauty and tranquillity that surrounded me, an ominous cloud of foreboding seemed to loom overhead. As I traversed the peaceful countryside, I couldn't shake the feeling of impending doom. Thoughts of my own mortality haunted me, and I couldn't help but believe that death was inching closer with every passing moment. The serenity had given rise to a haunting sense of existential dread.

As the sun began its descent, I reluctantly made my way back to the bus stop, prepared to return home. The villages had granted me the solitude I yearned for, but they hadn't fully dispelled the pervasive anxiety that had taken hold of me. The weight of my responsibilities in the digital world was hanging over me, and the apprehension of what I might find on my phone was gnawing at my soul.

The bus ride back was somber. I gazed out of the window, my thoughts consumed by a tumultuous mix of emotions. When I finally arrived home and retrieved my phone, it felt like stepping back into a different dimension. I switched it on, and it came alive with a barrage of notifications. The messages, emails, and missed calls had accumulated during my absence. The digital world had continued to spin, completely indifferent to my solitude. The sheer volume of information was overwhelming, and I felt more isolated than ever. I began sorting through the messages, but two in particular, stood out. One was a vague request for help from a friend, seeking assistance on a matter that seemed trivial in the grand scheme of things. The other was a message from another friend, a long-winded complaint about the minor inconveniences of their day. In that moment, it struck me how distant and insignificant these digital connections were.

As I responded to the messages, a profound sense of loneliness washed over me. I offered support and advice to my friends, and I empathized with the minutiae of their lives. But as I typed, I couldn't help but feel that the peace and quiet I had found on my unplanned journey had amplified my sense of isolation.

In my quest to escape the noise of the world, I had stumbled into a deeper, more profound loneliness. The villages and the people I had encountered had shown me the beauty of simplicity and the importance of slowing down, but they had also underlined the stark reality of solitude. And as I looked at my phone, I realized that true peace and quiet, amid the chaos, had left me feeling more alone and vulnerable than ever.

Day 7

– Acceptance of Pain –

Time stamp 17.00

The clock on the wall had barely ticked past 17:00 and I could feel the weight of an entire week's worth of anticipation pressing down on me. It had been a long week, one filled with anxiety, sleepless nights, and the haunting shadow of uncertainty. At my age and lack of experience, I was about to receive news that would change the course of my life forever. The fear that had gripped me for days was about to find a voice, and my journey through the world of chronic illness was about to begin. As the minutes crawled by, I found myself standing by the window, staring out at the world beyond. The sun was beginning its descent, casting long shadows and painting the sky with hues of orange and pink. It was a stark contrast to the storm of emotions raging within me. The phone call that I had been waiting for, the call from my doctor, was the answer to a question I never thought I'd have to ask. 17:15, I took a deep breath and answered, my voice was trembling with anxiety. The doctor's words were delivered with a solemnity that sent a chill down my spine. "I'm afraid it's confirmed," the doctor said, "you have a chronic illness. Your life may not be as long as you hoped, but there's still a lot to live for."

Those words hung in the air, heavy and full of implications. A part of me had anticipated this, but the reality of the diagnosis was something I had not fully prepared for. It felt as though I was being plunged into the depths of a dark and unfamiliar sea, struggling to find my footing in turbulent waters. Yet, despite the fear and despair, there was something else that stirred within me. A glimmer of hope, faint but undeniable. It was a stubborn voice deep inside, whispering that this was not the end, but a new beginning. The journey ahead would be different from anything I had ever known, but it was a journey I was determined to undertake.

The doctor explained the nature of my chronic illness, its impact on my body, and the changes that would be necessary to manage it and extend my life. The words were delivered with a mixture of compassion and professionalism, and I absorbed them like a sponge, determined to understand and accept my new reality. In the end, I felt a strange sense of relief. The uncertainty that had plagued me for the past week had been replaced by a clear path forward. My life had taken an unexpected turn, but it was still a life worth living. The diagnosis was not a death sentence, but a call to adapt, to change, and to fight for every day. I found myself making mental lists of the things I would need to do. Medications, lifestyle changes, and regular check-ups would become a permanent part of my life. It was a daunting prospect, but I was determined to face it head-on.

What kept me going, however, was not just the will to live for myself, but for those who had become my chosen family. Friends who had stood by me, offering their unwavering support and love, had become my lifeline. They were not mere friends; they were the family I had chosen, and their presence in my life had taken on a profound significance. I hope I will find strength in vulnerability, courage in the face of adversity, and resilience in the midst of uncertainty. There will be good days and bad days, but through it all, the love, support and sometimes annoying presence of my family, will hopefully sustain me. I know I might never learn to find joy in the small moments, to appreciate the beauty of each sunrise, and to cherish the laughter of my loved ones, but at least I might try to be there for them. My life had indeed taken an unexpected turn, and the road ahead was filled with twists and turns. But it was a road I was willing to travel, not just for myself, but for those who had become my reason to live. The end of this long week of waiting has marked a new beginning, and I'm determined to make the most of every moment, living not just for myself but for the family I had found along my way.

Bonus Chapter

My dear reader, my life is not over yet.

As evidenced by our discussion we carry purpose in all, of our activity, but do we carry meaning? Within this chapter I won't be brief but rather "ambigu". Chaotic as it might be, take this chapter as my long-lasting goodbye letter.

Now meaning is something beyond human explanation as in defying meaning we define faith, belief, commitment and strength. The biggest question of all time. If we can scratch, and I'll try my best to break the surface of this question "What is the meaning of ……?" of anything, of something, something that's mine or has never belonged to me, something such as life…… my life.

Can it be mine? Firstly, is it yours because you have it or because you use, or because you own control over it. Or does it belong to the maker, the mother and the father? My lack of faith and disbelief in religion limits my options of ownership to others just like me. With no being to own my life, the life inside of me is mine to endure, carry and reward. But what if there was a god? You my dear reader should have all the entitlement to believe in such things, beings, energies, etc. what if there was an original maker? Consider this god exists. God created life. Your life is a result of other creations which originate within him.

Not that difficult to imagine I assume. So, in this context let's relate this to a shoe. As why not imagine more than we already have. The maker of the shoe is the owner of its meaning, until it gets sold to a customer who wears the shoe. What is the meaning of the shoe, you might ask. Well to be used as a shoe and nothing more than what the maker intended. Going back to being sold to a customer, which might end putting the shoes in a charity box until a new owner comes along. Through use and tear the shoe will end, be disposed of, destroyed, repurposed, remembered. Consider this, while the maker made the shoe, it has not made its materials, therefore they have their own maker, their own god and yes, the shoe is life.

Have you considered my thought? And yet if the shoemaker is outsourcing materials, those become ancestors, providers of materials, become god until we change and lose focus of our question. What is the meaning of a life? The simple answer is No, not to the question above but to the question below. What is the meaning of a life without an owner? Going back to our shoes. Stuck in a box with no purpose, or owner (the same shoes which ended up in a charity box) in an abandoned warehouse or with a glimpse of hope for one day a saviour an owner may choose them and give them purpose, utilisation but not meaning(as meaning was already given by their maker, and it cannot be replaced, a shoe is a shoe and will remain one for the rest of its existence). Just like a child without parents, abandoned, alone, in a desperate long-lasting moment of waiting. The owner of a life does not give meaning, but allocates purpose regardless of being god, yourself or someone else.

We can conclude that within our imaginative exercise the owner does not matter. Therefore, removing it from the question simplifies the answer. To what is the meaning of a life. Let's simplify even further to "what is the meaning of life? In order to do so we need to attribute value through numbers to one's life (just so that we can remove the "a" / one life / idea of quantity). And if we succeed in concluding that life can be either a positive or negative number. We can then agree that we can measure it against other lives. If so, is the life of a child more valuable than 100? Regardless of Yes or No answers, what determines the value is what constructs the society that child lives in. (imagine the structure and culture which determines the value of an individual life) So this answer might differ, but the difference does not matter as long as the mechanism behind operates the same. In our thought-provoking imagination, we are giving value. Steve is better than Joe and George is worse than Michael. Since a value exists within our real-life system. (grades, pay scales etc) It cannot give meaning, but merely express a fraction of situational moments (a picture frozen in time). In which we can witness the afterimage of meaning through others' eyes.

Such systems which grade our life, do not offer meaning. They represent a set of cultural values, standards, and achievements that an individual's encounters during its lifetime. It is unfair to say that the meaning of a child's life is to achieve grade x in a discipline or an adult 's meaning is to produce x amount of money and pay x amount of taxes. Rather we can agree that a grade obtained by a child is just a moment (snapshot) of its entire life. Yet again we conclude that while we can attribute to life does not give meaning but does merely represent it. Yet again we simplify towards what is the meaning of life. We gratefully reach a conundrum of thoughts and theories to simplify further. Let's avoid that, let's not use a hammer more than what is needed. The remaining elements of "What", "meaning" and "life" are necessary to understand and explore our question. From simplification to breaking apart we will use a range of tools to deconstruct our knowledge. Let's start easy, "The What '' by asking a "what" question, which answers are we willing to accept. As it may be difficult to accept answers which are against our preconceived bias. Are we going to accept rational, emotional, numerical, interpretative or a confirmation of our bias. Our dilemma is not that we have a question, but that we have the answer to our question. We have always had the answer to this question but refused to accept it. It's often the case that we ask questions to validate or contradict our answers. Nothing more or less, it is our curiosity of moving from the "why?" as babies into the "what?" as adults. Let's not make an exception out of this, let's just say it the meaning of life is ……..

There you go, you fill in the gaps for yourself and let no-one tell you what you think is wrong with your meaning. If only it would be that easy, if all had the strength to be ourselves with no personal and interpersonal judgements. Or projections of who we are through other lenses ("What will x think?"). But it is not easy, so let's agree that regardless of the answer we might still have a series of questions to solidify or weaken our previous affirmation of truth. Basically, we might not agree based on our bias. Back to our question. What is the meaning of life? Let's define meaning. Better said, let's not confuse meaning with purpose. Purpose is the reason for which something gets done, therefore any reason which we might have to pursue a career to build a family, to be a better etc. This is not meaning, it's actually quite different from what meaning represents. Purpose is derived from our intention. With this said we can identify our first difference to meaning. Meaning is directly expressed, and is covert, hidden. Expressed and indicated by previous ideologies. By others, just like us, from different or same time with us, from the same or different space with us. (You should become a lawyer because xyz). Often implemented before our existence. (When my son grows up, he will be a footballer) Let's consider an example of our shoes where the purpose and the meaning converge for the shoes. Designed and created with purpose, to be worn, they fulfilled their meaning after being worn and gained purpose, given by their owner. Those are my running shoes. Same with a child before it gets born, his parents can only imagine what it can become, a doctor, a lawyer etc. But when the child grows older it's free to create its own purpose. Choose a different career than what his parents could have imagined. Therefore, meaning is something that could have been imagined before they created their individual purpose. Let's go back to our questions, as defining meaning under those terms turns the question dull. Unless you believe in god, and as you know i don't. But for the purpose of our conversation. Why would someone try to think if there is something more to life than a simple relationship between purpose (your own initiative/ individual agency) and meaning preconceived ideas based on different generations values/

previous cultural and structural norms). Therefore, if god is real, I'll let you expand on what was the intended meaning on someone's life.

Out of my own disbelief in god, I pursue this question out of curiosity, and it is for the scientific endeavour to refuse my null hypothesis. Think without assuming that my views are right or wrong. So, let's consider "meaning" under the following diagram which includes five elements: Time, Space, Culture, Structure and Individual Agency. Time is an interesting construct as by taking a snapshot of past events we can understand how those shape the priorities of a generation. To give an example, approximately 100 years ago the most important job was coal mining and other roles focused on manual labour. Completely different from today's society which is focused on roles requiring data literacy, critical thinking and tech savviness. But 100 years in the lifetime of a family is not much. In reflection is quite a small period of time. If we base our example on the average age of having a child (30 years old) and the average life expectancy (80 years old) in the UK. For an extended family with a newborn in 2023 it can engulf the views and values of parents and grandparents. Which on their own have experienced the views and values of their parents and grandparents. Past lifetime values reflect on the difference between older generations creating meaning for younger generations. In other words, you need to understand your past to understand where your future can go. A different factor, space or environment better defined, is a construct volatile to change over time. If you don't believe me, search for a photo for your place from 50 years ago. The term volatile, I use to underline that it responds to the community culture - structure - agency relationship. Which we will cover soon. There are pockets of spaces which have moved and progressed from 50 years ago. There are other pockets which have remained the same. But in both cases the space reflected the influence of culture - structure - agency relationship within its local community. To give an example, a town which has not changed much in the last 50 years, will hold to past values and create meaning for the lifestyle from 50 years ago. This can create a clash of generational values between older generations creating meaning and younger generation desiring a different purpose. Therefore, the place where one lives is an accumulation of values and beliefs of not only present but also past generations which contributed to today's social environment. Let's discuss culture. We spoke about time and environment, but it came time to speak about the elephant in the room.

The culture existing within an environment has the most impact over time on the intended meaning. Let's exemplify by looking at coastal towns with strong traditions of trading and producing jobs within the marine transport sector. Within this context, the culture of the environment focuses on stability and security (conservative values / maintaining the status quo), creating/ offering meaning relating back to structural opportunities within the marine transport sector (traditional values, traditional jobs aka my father has done this, his father has done this and so on). Structural opportunities link closely with cultural values of the community and create a live state of flux in which individuals with different / opposing cultural values struggle to find purpose (the town is alive, jobs will stay the same but will change individuals in charge of them over generations; there are no new titles and everyone is expected to follow in someone steps). This leaves individual agency in a different position in which the options are within the realm of assimilation or venture into a new environment. (Stay and conform to the values or leave your birthplace behind to discover something different). It is within this critical choice where individual agency, extremely limited, creates the distinction between meaning (the intended) and purpose (the created). Going back to our question "What is the meaning of someone's life?". It is every: thing, concept, desire, sweat and work dedicated to creating opportunities for that person's life. It can be what parents, with best intentions, who prepare every avenue for their children in order to ensure their safety and future stability. You my dear reader take my conclusion in any realist, religious and philosophical direction you want. Just remember that what you do with your life is defined as purpose as it is up to you to give your life purpose regardless of if it aligns with your meaning. Until next time, thank you.

Printed in Great Britain
by Amazon